HOW TO MAKE A **SIX-FIGURES AS**

A REAL ESTATE AGENT

AN EASY WAY TO MAKE MONEY AND GET PEOPLE
TO TAKE YOU SERIOUSLY AS A PROFESSIONAL

RAMONICA R. CALDWELL

ISBN-10: 0692976337
ISBN-13: 978-0692976333

DEDICATION

*I would like to dedicate this book to motivated
real estate professionals that are ready
to become successful
and are eager to make money in real estate*

And

*A special thanks to friends, family, past clients, current clients,
and future clients for without you I would have no success
to write about.*

ACKNOWLEDGEMENTS

1. Michael Brown
2. Chelsea Malone
3. Terry Forde
4. Crystal Davis
5. Daniel Holliday
6. Brian Ford
7. Ria Harris
8. ShaRhonda Hill
9. Alexia Sims
10. Shamika Jones
11. Akindele Akinyemi
12. Lamont Tolliver
13. Cortney Gee
14. DeSean Yates
15. Norman Rudolph Jr.
16. Delicia Lacy
17. Samyka Leaston-Pinkney
18. Byron Lundy
19. Tomeka Givens
20. Manning Bertrand Realty Investments LLC
21. Rosalie Silva
22. Blue Touch Pool Service
23. Geraldine Salazar
24. Leigh Johnson
25. Joy Harrell
26. Karen's Make Ready Services
27. Nicole Handy
28. Elisa Hanson-Linton
29. Sheila Collins
30. Khalida Bennett
31. Kandie Martin
32. Barry Bolston
33. Brandon Killian
34. Lonzdrea Allen
35. Darryle Holloway-Hughes
36. Tavarious Robinson
37. God's Girl Fashion
38. Ryan Terry
39. Donivan Harvey
40. LaDonna Parker
41. Madeira Hatcher
42. Kalombo Kayeme
43. Ovit Pursley
44. Terry Mucker
45. Rebuild Beaumont (Divine Residential Services)
46. Michelle Johnson
47. Levert Caldwell
48. Thomas Amal
49. Bruce Ham
50. VMS Communications
51. Sabrina Ash
52. Aurelia Wagner
53. Phillip Dunn (Black Business Focus Group)
54. Venessa James
55. Joy Diggs
56. Angela Jarvis
57. Success Tax Relief, Inc. (Thelma Coleman)
58. Lamik Beauty
59. Hanifa Staine
60. Amber Burton Consulting
61. SPARC Solutions

CONTENTS

PREFACE

When I started in real estate I thought it was going to be an easy job. I thought I would make millions overnight or at least "in the next 5 years"! You laugh but I was serious! I learned the hard way how untrue that was. My original income goal as a real estate agent was to replace my annual salary of $50,000 as a teacher. Eventually my goals grew to wanting to earn "six-figures". To be honest, six-figures was more than I thought I could ever earn. See, I was raised in a family of hourly wage workers so making a teacher's salary was a "step up". With a $50,000 annual salary, I was already earning thousands of dollars more in yearly income than many in my immediate family.

So mistakenly I thought I "made it", until I started to feel the pressure my monthly bills put on my salary. I felt like I was literally living "paycheck to paycheck" even though I was earning a "good" living. At that point, I felt duped. I felt like I didn't go to college and work hard to be burdened bills and still have a "paycheck to paycheck" life! One day, I got an idea in my head. I had a strong desire to make more than just $50,000 per year as a Teacher. It sounds crazy now! But I dreamed that I could make more. I dreamed that I could make $100,000 or more. I didn't have a literal dream I had a very strong desire that was stuck in my head and it wouldn't leave. So I started thinking of ways to get out of the rat race to make that dream happen. Real estate was a long-time passion, so I got licensed, worked my butt off and one day, my dream came true. It took me a couple years but I began earning over $100k in real estate as a full-time practitioner without having a full-time job. This book was conceived through a similar process, one day I had a idea that I could create content for agents like myself that see themselves earning more in their real estate career and want to do the work to make it happen.

Frankly, I wrote this book to introduce agents to the reality of real estate, the work that is required to be successful, the types of topics you should be well-versed in as a real estate salesperson, how to represent yourself as a professional and what tools you need in place to make your job easier and earn you more money. These are all factors that make an agent a Superstar but are often understated or overlooked. I wrote this book for agents that care about their career and making money. I believe in you! And I believe many agents like you want to know and need to know how to make money in real estate sales! So, use this book as a lesson and proof that if I can earn six figures, so can you!

CHAPTER 1

WHY READ THIS BOOK?

"The most important step of all is the first step.
Start something." — Blake Mycoskie

How to Make Six-Figures is a little different than other real estate books. Other real estate books teach you how to dominate your market, beat out the competition, and become a beast at a specific real estate strategy. I have found tons and tons of real estate content that teach how to call on Expired Listings, how to call on For Sale by Owners, how to host kick-ass Open Houses and 100+ other ways to make you successful as a real estate professional. However, I have found very little information on how to build up a platform where you will be seen as a professional. Hence, that's the motivation for my book. I simply started with a six-figure income goal because it's the most common goal for most people. Sometimes it's easier to take a small bite out of a slice of pie rather than eat the whole slice. How to Make Six-Figures allows you to take a bite out of a slice of pie.

Here's something we have all heard before "As a real estate agent, you will wear many hats". Even though it may sound cliche', it's true! Real estate is unlike any other industry. It's different than any other sales job because from day one, you are the business. There's no Assistant, there's no salary, there's no call list of warm leads, cold leads, or hot leads. YOU as an Independent Contractor are responsible for creating everything that will make your business a success. The best way to start creating that success is by taking your career seriously from the beginning. Start your career with an understanding that there are many functions of "the job" that you are personally responsible for not your broker. Be prepared to market and highlight unique qualities about yourself, generate leads on your own, know how to convert leads, learn to negotiate and write contracts, properly fill out listing paperwork and buyer paperwork, get comfortable with sales techniques like closing buyers and sellers. Knowing what is required of you as a professional, drives your focus and direction. Your focus helps you become more credible and marketable to your clients.

In my experience, there are very few authorities teaching how to master and market yourself as a professional. *How to Make Six-Figures* focuses on the development of your identity as a real estate professional. I am going to show you how to approach your career so that you attract a beneficial sphere of influence, build credibility, and be seen as a competent real estate professional. Because this book is written by a practicing real estate broker logically some "how-tos" about the "real estate job" are going to be sprinkled throughout the book, even though that is not the primary focus of the book.

Prior to earning six-figures, I observed agents on every level. I studied real estate agents that sold over 1,000 homes per year to those that have sold only one home in the last twelve months. The observations with the greatest impact were of successful agents. However, struggling agents moved me to write this book. When I was a struggling agent, I would call up other struggling agents to compare notes to see "why were we struggling?". It seems funny now but at the time that was my life. When I stopped struggling and became more successful, I started to ask well "what did I do differently?" Then I reflected on previous conversations and I remembered all of the negative things I had in my head. I would have conversations like "It's hard", "I don't know what to do", or "I tried that, but it didn't work". The first thing I did was stopped believing the negative thoughts. Next, I made a commitment to learning as much as possible.

When I meet agents today, I ask "what's you holding back"? Not surprisingly, I hear the same negative concerns I once had. After chatting with enough agents, I realized there is still an unmet need to help agents succeed. I decided to write a book that makes it easy to understand what it takes to make money in real estate as an agent. The goal for this book is to include as much practical advice as possible that will work for any real estate agent no matter where they are in their career!

REALITY CHECK

Another valuable reason to read this book is because when I started in real estate I thought it would be super easy to do the work of a real estate agent. My goal was to make a $100,000 per year. The goal of $100K seemed astronomical. All I kept thinking was: this is going to be easy because I am a hard worker, I mean how hard can it be? All I am doing as agent is showing houses, right? What's so hard about that? On top of that the seller is going to pay me thousands of dollars for showing houses for a couple of hours. Where do I sign up for that gig? I soon realized the task was much bigger than the expectation.

As I got more experienced, I soon realized $100,000 was a small income goal in the total context of real estate. If no one has told you or you haven't thought big enough yet, you can make much more than six-figures in real estate. The beauty of being a real estate professional is that you can **make more than** a six-figure income. Maybe you are not as naïve as I was, and you already know this. But a first step to earning more is believing that you can earn more. Know that your real estate income goals should be *unlimited*!

It may sound strange, but the reason I repeated the thought process of making more and unlimited income so many times is because this was an important concept for me to understand. I was so limited in only seeing a way to replace my teacher's salary that I didn't even think about earning more than six-figures. And trust me there is plenty more than six-figures to be made in a real estate career. After reading this book, you will learn how to position yourself as an expert, present a professional image and effectively communicate your value as a real estate professional and start making a six-figure income or more in no time!

CHAPTER 2
THE BASICS

"Fundamentals, Fundamentals, Fundamentals.
You've got to get the fundamentals down because
otherwise the fancy stuff isn't going to work."
— Randy Pausch

The Basics of real estate addresses the fundamentals of real estate that every agent should know. Being in real estate for many years, I have heard many perspectives on the role of a real estate agent. As I work with more clients, I realize many people don't understand what a "real estate agent" actually does. Personally, I believe that is a huge part of the problem of why real estate agents have a hard time "selling" themselves. Not only does the consumer not understand what we do as agents, but oftentimes real estate agents themselves do not understand their role or job in a real estate transaction.

In fact, if you follow the top 1% of real estate professionals as I have, you will hear Top Producing agents caution 'inexperienced' agents about the importance of communicating value as a real estate agent. You hear Top Producing agents coach on to topics like "Don't Reduce Your Fees", "Communicate Value to Your Clients", "Come from a place of Contribution" and so forth.

The best of the best agents regularly critique the industry and suggest we as real estate professionals need to clearly communicate our value proposition. I must admit I agree I believe these industry leaders see a huge gap being unfulfilled and they offer their coaching and advice as warnings to us true professionals. In short, we as professionals need to do a better job explaining our work. I think one reason the public — our consumers, do not understand our role and sometimes even disregard our value as a real estate professional is because we have not done a good enough job communicating our role and value to the consumer. In my opinion, the public, or consumers lack of understanding of our role as a real estate professionals is due to our failure to clearly communicate why buyers should hire an agent and sellers should hire an agent. If no one can clearly communicate why to hire a professional agent other than to "get my house on the market" then it becomes increasingly harder to believe that you even need a professional to "sell your home". In my opinion lack of value leads to or fuels the fire for For Sale By Owners or $395 Flat Listing Service companies to exist. When they become the norm, this tells us the marketplace is not recognizing value in having a real estate agent and thus the market is responding accordingly.

As agents sometimes we are too hungry for business that we neglect to provide a high quality service. Sometimes we are so excited about an opportunity to work with a buyer or seller that we take off running without fully evaluating the type of business we are chasing or the service we are providing. This eagerness to work for any and every one, leads to confusion and lack of professionalism. As professionals we must have clear goals, expectations and purpose in our real estate dealings. Every service-based business has some form of clarity and direction. Real estate should not be any different. Think of when you go to visit your Hair Stylist, Barber, or Personal Trainer, etc. Your objectives are usually clearly expressed, right? When working with a professional Hair Stylist, you are choosing between getting a haircut, hair color or styling, or some special treatment for your hair. When working with your Personal Trainer you are choosing to either lose weight, tone muscle, or strengthen muscle for your body type. In an appointment with your barber, you are likely trimming your hair or shaping your beard. Any professional you work with starts with an idea or game plan. Then typically the professional takes the lead in guiding you in the right direction so that you get the results you want. Real estate works the same way. When we start working with a client we should be leading by identifying their goals then guiding them in the right direction.

There's a difference between being a professional and an order taker. An order taker is led by the prospect, the customer tells the order taker what they want and the order taker delivers. A professional on the other hand leads the customer. A professional asks what are your goals? What are you attempting to achieve? Then the customer shares what they plan to accomplish and what they hope to gain from a working relationship with the professional. Then the professional takes on the role and guides the prospect in the right direction to achieve the desired result. Sometimes real estate professionals are looked at as "order takers" versus the professional advisors we are trained to be. Address this early in your career, start with knowing your role so that you are always respected as a professional advisor not an order taker.

Unsurprisingly, this is the reason why experienced agents argue that the average real estate agent lacks training, skill, and professionalism. Have you ever heard the saying real estate agents are nothing more than a Used Car Salesman? Isn't that shocking? When I first heard this, I cringed! Then reality set in, I held a "salespersons" license. I learned to accept the baggage that came with that title which included respecting others opinions and body language. Even though it made me uncomfortable that potential customers cringed when I introduced myself as a real estate agent, I couldn't disregard the fact that they saw me as a "salesperson". I couldn't be offended when I was simply saying "Hello" at a networking event and instead of saying "Hello" back people would shout out, "I just bought a house!" As if I were going to pull out a sales contract and force them to sign it. From this experience, I learned that some people fear "salespeople". It has very little to do with you as a person and more to do with your role as a "salesperson". More to do with how they view different professions. Instead of being bummed out by how the public views you, get thicker skin. If you do not have tough skin, it can be frightening to think that people view you as a pushy salesperson without evening knowing you. This fear can be a definite confidence killer. So get over it quickly.

You can't win every battle with the public but you can position yourself in a way that separates you from the rest. If you don't want to be considered a pushy salesperson, learn better ways to market your skills and services. Become better at clearly communicating your role as the professional when working with clients. Also, we must become better at clearly stating our role as a professional when working with clients buying or selling real estate. Let's take a moment to get clear on what a real estate professional does in our various capacities.

Check out the Classification below by the National Association of REALTORS® so that you can effectively communicate the responsibilities of various real estate roles.

REAL ESTATE PROFESSIONAL ROLES

The National Association of Realtors[1] described each real estate professional's role as:

- ▶ **Real estate agent**: Anyone who earns a real estate license can be called a real estate agent, whether that license is as a sales professional, an associate broker or a broker. State requirements vary, but in all states, you must take a minimum number of classes and pass a test to earn your license.

---

1   Source: By Michele Lerner | Mar 10, 2014 – National Association of REALTORS®

- ▶ **REALTOR®**: A real estate agent who is a member of the National Association of REALTORS®, which means he or she must uphold the standards of the association and its code of ethics.
- ▶ **Real estate broker**: A person who has taken education beyond the agent level as required by state laws and has passed a broker's license exam. Brokers can work alone, or they can hire agents to work for them.
- ▶ **Real estate salesperson**: Another name for a real estate agent.
- ▶ **Real estate associate broker**: Someone who has taken additional education classes and earned a broker's license but chooses to work under the management of a broker.

After professional distinctions have been made and roles have been clearly defined, we can tell our clients how an agent is different from a broker. We can explain to our consumers the difference between a real estate agent and a REALTOR®. We must acknowledge that the titles, job descriptions, and responsibilities seem very similar. We must admit it can be confusing. Consumers don't always know the difference and oftentimes a lot of the titles are used interchangeably so that makes it even more complicated for those outside of the industry. To most people we are all "'real estate agents" or REALTORS®. The average consumer doesn't take the time to understand the difference between a real estate agent and a REALTOR®. It's important as professionals that we communicate the distinctions because in some cases classifications can make the difference in your experience level and skill set, such as broker compared to agent. Or REALTOR® compared to real estate agent. When we explain these differences, we must understand the value we are communicating and how it can differentiate us.

UNDERSTANDING YOUR VALUE AS AN AGENT

Your value can be divided in two parts: (1) knowledge from direct experience (2) knowledge from indirect experience. Indirect experience is gained through familiarity with a variety of real estate transactions. As your experience grows so does your expertise. You develop know-how overtime, use your awareness of what's happening in the industry to educate your buyers and sellers. Don't be afraid to share successes and failures. When you share what's happening you create value, you become recognized as an expert because you have the knowledge. Be prepared to share horror stories as well as happy stories with your clients. Remember that all of your experience does not have to be gained by you as an individual. Gain knowledge from other professionals around you, learn from their successes and failures. As you close transactions, note the experiences and lessons learned. Be prepared to share those experiences with your next set of clients. Each transaction could offer invaluable wisdom. Share your observations with future clients and prospects. Being "in the know" is an undeniable benefit to your clients.

A past client helped me recognize our value as real estate professionals. My client candidly shared "I come to you because I am at work all day and you are out in the field, so I expect you to know what's going on in the community I am thinking of living in". After our talk, I realized I had a huge responsibility to my clients, I realized that the expectations placed on my role as a real estate agent were bigger than I thought.

Our clients expect us to be aware of what's happening in the market. So I encourage you to make it your business to know what's happening in your market area. Our clients trust and depend on our expertise, they hire us for our expertise, we are their eyes into the real estate industry because we are the experts that study it while they focus on their job. Our greatest value as a real estate professional is an insight into the real estate world. We get to share what's really happening.

Looking at the bigger picture, you will notice that your role as a real estate professional is important because you are gaining invaluable experience every day. You are not gaining theoretical experience, you are gaining real-life practical knowledge every time you attend a closing, show a house, pull comps, and every time you submit a contract for negotiation. You are continuously gaining experience on a regular basis. Trust the experience that you have.

Don't be discouraged by consumers that pretend to be "real estate experts" from watching HGTV, the news, or hearsay from friends and family. Despite what you may hear by the consumer, the everyday laymen does not understand real estate the way they claim they understand real estate. Even though some consumers may go toe-to-toe to challenge your authority, the fact of the matter is that many people just don't get real estate. Ask yourself: if it was that easy, why aren't there more licensed real estate professionals? Or why do many real estate licensees quit after just 1 year? Or why are the Top Producers only 1% of the real estate population?

Don't take my word for it, look at the statistics the National Association of REALTORS® 2016 Profile of Home Buyers and Sellers, it states that 89% of sellers use an agent to sell their home. Often individuals that attempt to sell their home on their own ultimately end up hiring a real estate agent to sell their home. So, ask yourself, if selling real estate was not a skilled profession why do sellers need to hire a professional nearly 90% of the time to fulfill the job for them?

We should understand that selling a home without professional guidance may be fun for some people while challenging for others. However, either way it's safe to assume that most people selling a home on their own is probably a once-in-a-lifetime occurrence. On the other hand, a real estate agent has the opportunity to sell 20 homes per year, 50 homes per year or even over a 100+ homes per year regularly because it's part of the job. Naturally, there's a benefit to hiring a professional with proven experience opposed to working as a hobby every once in awhile.

Confidence aids you in being unmoved by a seller's disregard for your value. One person that sells one home occasionally should not invoke fear and devalue your role as a professional. With market knowledge facts you become invaluable as a real estate agent and can confidently market your expertise and strengths as a real estate professional.

It is our duty to effectively communicate knowledge and expertise to our clients, consumers, and prospects buying and selling real estate. Your unique experience with many types of real estate transactions gives you an edge over the consumer and creates value for you as real estate professional.

WHY INDUSTRY PROFESSIONALISM IS IMPORTANT

Think of your Dentist, Attorney, or CPA; when you meet with them, what's the standard? Do you have to call in advance? Can you get them on the phone right away? Is there a fee required? We must conduct our real estate practice with professionalism like other professionals have done to earn the respect of the public.

Too often, I have seen real estate professionals acting as City Tour Guides and less like a skilled professional agent.

Have you ever gotten a call from a client that just drove by a "For Sale" sign in a yard and called the agent's office on the sign demanding someone come show them the house right away? If you have had this experience, did you drop everything and go? This "on call" behavior demonstrates the actions of a *City Tour Guide*. A Tour Guide is defined as a person employed to show tourists around places of interest. As a standard of practice in their work, Tour Guides are usually readily available, sitting idly by, just waiting on tourists to pop-in and schedule a tour. When the phone rings or the door opens, the Tour Guide jumps to attention ready to get going with the customer and the tour. No questions asked, except maybe which tour would you like? Consider this, the last time you had a toothache, could you rush right in to see your Dentist? Or did you have to call to schedule an appointment and hope to high heavens your dentist wasn't booked? If you had to book an appointment know matter how important your issue was that's a sign you are working with a professional. Your Dentist, CPA, or attorney is usually not on standby waiting for your call unless you compensate them very well. Not that these professionals are not there when you need them, but they have a standard of service, a way of doing business. It is assumed that an office visit is necessary if you want service, an appointment or consultation is typically required, and their advice is usually highly regarded.

Real estate agents on the other hand fail to set a standard of service. The most valuable thing you can do for yourself to ensure that you earn a six-figure income is set a standard of service. Start telling your clients how your business works, tell them how they should contact you, how are appointments set up, when is a good time to call you. Avoid the eager beaver mentality. Don't rush to meet with buyers or sellers as an eager agent ready to serve. Instead enter your appointments as a professional prepared to assess the seller's or buyer's needs. I know what you may be thinking, "but we work for our clients." Yes, it is true we work for our clients. It is also true that we serve a greater role. Our role as fiduciaries, gives us a higher authority in relationships with our clients. As a fiduciary we advocate for our clients and are supposed to establish relationships built on trust, so that we will protect our clients' best interest.

Therefore, we need our clients to understand "how we do business", what representation is, and how loyalty applies. We must explain why working with a real estate agent is a benefit to them. If you are truly protecting your clients' best interest, you ask questions, you screen and qualify them, you make sure you understand the needs of your client.

Don't drop everything and run at a request of a client, prospect or customer. Showing a client house after house without even verifying if the client is financially capable of purchasing the home is unprofessional and under serving your client. It is our job to be professional agents. Professionalism goes a long way. In short, professionalism means to screen, qualify, assess, and explain your business practice to all consumers with whom you interact.

WHAT CONSUMERS LOSE IF AGENTS ARE NOT AROUND

Some consumers feel that real estate agents are not necessary. This could be because they are not aware of the risk posed to them by a buyer or seller or they could be underestimating the value of an agent. Again, it's our job as real estate professionals to show the importance of having an agent involved in the transaction. I know much talk has taken place about "real estate agents" being replaced by the Internet, but I strongly doubt that will happen. My disbelief in replacing real estate agents with technology simply lies in the fact that residential real estate is a people-based industry. In fact, residential real estate is largely based on people and emotions.

As you know, residential real estate is centered around family decisions. Think about it, our client-base is the family that must move because work is relocating them to another state. Our client-base are families selling a home due to divorce. Our client-base are newlyweds buying their first home together, or the single mom purchasing her first home for her children. As we look at these scenarios, we can see that each person will have a different set of challenges when it comes to their real estate transaction. Some of these challenges families face will require a "human experience". In emotional times, families will want to work with a professional that they can trust. This is where agents have a unique opportunity to sell yourself and your skill set. Families will need, and want, a human to walk them through the process of tough decisions. As a real estate professional, if you are focused on helping your client and explaining to them how you can make their transition through life easier you will have a long-lasting career. In my opinion, it is highly unlikely that a family will want to sell their home on their own in times of emotional turmoil. Can you imagine trying to sell your home online after the death of a spouse, parent or child? Of course not, you will likely want a professional service available.

Sometimes emotional situations arise when selling homes. As professional real estate agents, we can't undervalue these emotional times and how they also drive our business. Imagine if you are selling due to a death in your family, divorce, financial trouble, etc. Who do you want to help you with this? A real estate agent that you trust, or would you want to spend an hour or two on a computer trying to fill out complicated paperwork? More than likely, you would want someone you could entrust your most precious asset, your home. You would want to hire an agent that was sensitive to your family matters and exhibited a high level of professionalism to help you get through the process. We as agents must sell this as the experience and value that we bring to the table. Unfortunately, I think many consumers and real estate professionals alike misjudge the relevance and importance of why real estate professionals are valuable. Imagine, buying your first home, would you want to spend countless hours Internet surfing, looking at thousands of pictures, trying to figure out which neighborhood is best, before you make the decision to buy? Or would your home buying process be simpler if you had an agent you could trust give you the steps necessary to move forward with your purchase? I can tell you from experience that online home shopping may sound good at first, but it can be very frustrating. Think of how you feel when you get automated messages from call centers when you are trying to handle an important issue. If you are like me, you pray a human being picks up. Personally, I couldn't imagine surfing the Internet for hours on end trying to find a home because "I can do it on my own". Does that mean that all buyers will feel frustrated by an online process or want to work with a real estate agent? Of course not. Surely, there will be buyers that enjoy the DIY (do-it-yourself) approach and that's okay. Experience has shown me that some matters in real estate are just too complicated to be solved through DIY solutions. I could be wrong, and I am no psychic. However, I strongly believe that buyers and sellers will continue to want to hire real estate professionals in the future and DIY cannot replace an entire industry of service-based professionals.

Besides the emotional connection consumers may experience with a real estate agent, there is the ethical security that real estate professionals offer. Imagine for a moment, if agents did not exist, instead sellers and buyers dealt directly with each other for the purchase and sell process of real estate. Who would be the third party to supervise both sides? Whom would provide checks and balances? How many laws would we have to institute keep each party in the transaction honest? A key element of the real estate agent's job is a position of trust, recall the fiduciary responsibility? A real estate agent is often an objective voice in the transaction.

Yearly, we have numerous lawsuits surrounding real estate transactions. These lawsuits still take place regularly even with real estate agents in place, imagine what our court dockets would look like without ethical practices in place or real estate agents as third parties with objectivity? Would our system even be able to handle the case load of lawsuits between buyer and seller? Or Landlord and Tenant? Or builder and buyer? Or buyer and builder? The list can go on and on. From my experience, I can confidently tell you many For Sale by Owner (FSBO) sellers often don't know what paperwork is required to sell a home. And FSBO listings pop up every day online. How alarming is that? There are buyers readily buying homes from individuals that have not even issued the proper disclosures about their home. Clearly, I am not saying all FSBO operate this way. In fact, I don't know the specifics of how many do versus don't. I am simply making a point that in today's times there are some buyers and some sellers buying real estate without a thorough understanding of the risk they are exposing themselves to. They are taking this risk unbeknownst to them because they have declined the help of a real estate professional. What if this were the norm? Wouldn't it be a scary marketplace for real estate?

On the other hand, first time home buyers could be at a huge risk as well. If you have ever spoken with a first-time home buyer you'd learn right away they rarely know anything about buying real estate. They are often unaware of the process of preapproval, appropriate credit score, down payment needed and closing costs necessary to close on the home. Think of what our industry would look like if real estate agents were not in the picture and these buyers were in the marketplace on their own looking for a home. Are you starting to see the value of having a career as a professional real estate agent? Buyers and sellers need guidance. Whether they want to admit it or not is a topic for the ages. Our goal as professionals is to show them our value and communicate it effectively until they realize they can't live without us. Agents that do this will earn six-figures or more in income and will always be in demand as a real estate professional.

My suggestion is to effectively communicate your value, your role and your responsibilities to consumers. Show your prospects, consumers, and clients why you are important. Start brainstorming ways to create value in the marketplace by asking yourself "what are my clients trusting me with?" When I did this activity, I found that my clients were trusting me to protect their financial interest, their real estate interest and their legal interest in all real estate dealings. Use your thoughts and ideas to help start creating your brand & value proposition.

I encourage you to see your role as a profession not a job, consider your value being more important than simply scheduling an appointment to view homes or putting a listing in the MLS. Convince your clients that you are the best agent to protect their interest. Don't be afraid to answer the question of "Why, should I hire you as my agent?" Knowing your role and what you offer can help answer this question confidently to sell yourself. In case a suitable answer, slipped by you from above, your answer should demonstrate benefits to the buyer or seller. A good place to start would be highlighting your objectivity, fiduciary responsibility, and the service you offer clients to resolve emotional or complex problems. Certainly, it would be a good idea to communicate to your clients and prospects how you guard their financial, legal, and real estate interest.

CHAPTER 3

PREPARE YOUR MIND FOR SUCCESS

"Our only limitations are those that we set up in our own minds." — Napoleon Hill

After studying dozens of successful people, you will hear talk about this phenom called "mindset". Frankly, I have heard it so much I get sick of it. Then, just when I think I have had enough of it, a little voice will pop up in my head when I am being unproductive and say change your "mindset". If you are unfamiliar, mindset is simply an attitude or belief about something. I won't pretend to be a "Guru" at changing mindsets. Trust me, I am far from being a Tony Robbins, so I am not going to dive deeply into this topic. However, I will say what you think has a huge part on how you act and what you are willing to do. If you think small, you will create small opportunities. If you think big, you will create big opportunities. Later on in this book, you will find a *Resources* section where I list some incredible Motivational Speakers that are experts at explaining how to get more out of you and how to push yourself to be greater by changing the way you think. These speakers will allow you to get familiar with personal development and changing your "mindset". Although, I wouldn't call myself a Motivational Speaker, I am addressing mindset in this book because it influences how we conduct business and the choices we make. From a real-world point-of-view, I will share important mindset tips I applied to my life to help me make six-figures as a real estate agent. If it worked for me, it will work for you.

HERE'S HOW I CHANGED MY MINDSET

62. Accepted the Fact that Work Is Required

When I got into real estate, I thought it was going to be easy! Believe me, I really did. Since, I knew how to write a real estate sales contract, had previously worked as a real estate assistant, knew a little about houses because my dad was a carpenter, and I knew how to talk to people because I had some telemarketing experience, I thought I was going to be the bomb.com at real estate. Excuse me, while I catch myself from choking on laughter! It still tickles me to this day that this was my reality! I seriously believed it would be easy to "just sell houses".

Now, I can tell you from experience and tough lessons learned that it is not as easy as it sounds. Sure, your life experience prepares you in some ways. Certainly, you may be able to use some of the skills developed in other industries to help support your career in real estate. However, there is much more work required in real estate than you may be anticipating. The role of a real estate agent entails more than writing contracts, putting a listing in the MLS, and talking to people. Despite what you may read or see, real estate is made to look very easy by professionals. We should give credit were credit is due because some of the top professionals in the industry make it look way too easy. The truth is the highly successful real estate agents have put in hard work. Some of the skills we take for granted are the ability to be able to create a relationship of trust with a buyer or seller. Think this over for a moment. In our industry we get complete strangers to sign contracts with us for hundreds of thousands of dollars. If you unpack that, that's a high level skill. We should all give ourselves a pat on the back when we make that happen. In the grand scheme of things that is a huge marketable skill! That is no easy task. Real estate allows you as a complete stranger to become a part of a clients family, give advice on personal finances, credit and home choice. Your clients trust your opinion and feedback when it comes to important decisions about their home environment. To build that kind of confidence and trust is not easy.

Behind every great agent is a skill set that they have mastered. You may notice an agent in your market that lists all the homes for the Builders in your area or this agent may list every home in a geographic subdivision, behind that success I can assure you were countless hours or prospecting, lead generation and/or marketing dollars spent to solidify the agent's position. One day, I stopped and asked myself what is Sally Sue Agent doing that I am not, I see her signs everywhere? How is Jean Doe getting all these listings? Oh, that was a very nice open house, I wonder how they got sponsors to help host it? I got very inquisitive and started noticing what other agents were actually doing instead of complaining about why I was not succeeding. I recommend if you want to start producing more income, start thinking of ways that you can start working more to get better results. Don't be naive like I was, instead buckle down and grind. Figure out what work needs to be done. Adjust your mindset and attitude to one of "I can do this, and get it done"!

63. Connect with your Sphere of Influence

The first thing you need to know about any sales position is that people must like you, know you and trust you. Real estate is no different. The faster you can get connected to people that know, like, and trust you the quicker you can start to increase your contacts and likely future business. If you have been disconnected for whatever reason, start renewing your relationships by reconnecting. Re-establish relationships with people that may support you including past employers, co-workers, colleagues, civic club members, professional associations, sororities, fraternities etc. Where ever you have built up a network of people that know you, like you, and trust you, it's time to reconnect and get reacquainted. Having familiar relationships will be somewhat easier for you when asking for and promoting your service as a real estate agent. When was the last time you asked from business from your Sphere of Influence? A sphere of influence is made up of people you know. Each of us is connected to a unique audience. Perhaps you are connected to a friend from church that just moved into to town and wants to buy a home? Or you have golfing buddy that's looking to move a little closer to his favorite Golf Course? Maybe your Yoga Instructor wants to sell their home to use the extra funds to expand their Yoga business? Regardless of where you make connections, it's important that you strengthen or establish relationships with your Sphere of Influence. Your sphere of influence are your warm prospects. This is a starting point for building your business. Start to make a list of names of people you know. An important thing to keep in mind is that you need to "be nice" to everyone, you never know what relationships or people you may cross in the future that will want to buy, sell or even invest in real estate. Keep in mind everyone needs a place to live, your nemesis today may be a buyer or seller in 10-12 years. If you don't have a network, it's time to build one.

64. Seek Mentorship

Mentorship is necessary when wanting to grow professionally. Personally, I didn't understand the value of mentorship until many years after being a licensed agent. Unfortunately, when I started out as an agent I was to bull-headed and individualistic as a person, I thought I didn't need any help. The one thing that saved me from being a total disaster of stupidity was the fact that I was wise enough to surround myself with agents smarter than I was. I followed extremely successful real estate agents and learned from them. It's funny, when I look back now, I see many mistakes that could have been avoided if I had took mentorship seriously when I first got licensed.

Eventually, I started learning from those that were doing better than I was and taking direction from them. One thing I learned was that mentorship doesn't have to be assigned to one mentor nor does it have to be a formal arrangement. Mentors are individuals that you learn from and that guide you to develop professionally and/or personally. You can establish a mentoring relationship anyway you see fit as long as the person you want to serve as a mentor agrees. If you don't have an in-person mentor consider a virtual arrangement, choose someone that is very well experienced and has lots of content available online where you can learn virtually. Personally, I didn't have any particular person take me under their wing and say: "I am going to mentor you and make you the best real estate agent." I took the lead in my career and found good candidates that I felt were the models of what I wanted to accomplish. I followed them virtually until I got the desired results I wanted. I still use virtual mentorship today.

Seeking out and following Top Producing Agents and leaders in the real estate industry eventually rubs off on you and your business starts to improve. You'd be surprised at how much knowledge you gather when you follow the best of the best. Looking for a mentor? Check out blogs, podcast, YouTube, Facebook, or Instagram. There are some very highly successful agents that use these platforms to connect with audiences that want their help. Find them and start learning from them today. Perhaps, they may have even written a book or two that can help you start growing your real estate business. There are many ways to get mentorship, choose the one that works best for you. Seek a Mentor that you aspire to be.

65. Visualize Your Business

Write down your vision for your business. Do you see yourself selling 50+ homes a year, 100+ homes per year, a 1,000+ homes a year, or maybe you just want to sell one home per month? What's your vision for your business? Create your vision as big or as small as you'd like. I have hundreds of notes on lined paper, copy paper, post-its and note pads. I even record visions or thoughts on my voice recorder on my phone. My vision of my business gets clearer and clearer over time. Your vision may or may not be crystal clear at the start of your career. However, the most important work you can do is to simply make sure you have a vision for where your real estate career is going. Be candid with yourself. When you think of yourself as a real estate agent, what's the vision you see? How are you dressed? Who are you working with? What are you driving? What does your office look like? These are the types of questions you want to ask to help guide your business direction.

It's important to always look introspectively at how you view the world. Think about what's happening in the world around you as well. Adjusting your mindset is the first step in that direction. In this chapter, we discussed the true work ethic required to sell real estate, how your sphere of influence can be an asset to you, the importance of seeking a mentor and lastly visualizing your business. Key actions you should take after reading this chapter are: (1) Find someone on a higher level to mimic their success (2) Study successful people in and outside of real estate (3) Listen daily to Coaches about mindset, wealth, and habits (4) Write out your vision for your business.

Earn your six-figures with proper planning and preparation.

CHAPTER 4

PROJECT
A PROFESSIONAL
IMAGE

"The Presentation and Packaging is Everything."
— Eric Davis

Your persona, pictures, and appearance are important as a real estate agent it is how the world sees you. In describing your image, I am referring to overall presentation— how you show up in pictures, in dress & style to events, and in person before buyers and sellers. Your image plays a huge role in how you connect with people. I remember having lunch with a mentor several years ago, I asked "what could I do to attract a higher level of clients?". Surprisingly, I was bluntly advised to "dress better". After lunch, the statement replayed in my head over and over again. I appreciated the tough love advice. It made me reflect on how I presented myself to the world.

Oftentimes when I see real estate agents in person their image is often different than what is represented on their business card or public sites. It is important to realize that your clients are looking to connect with an authentic person. The more recognizable you are the more likely clients are to trust you. Being identifiable helps build trust with your audience. If they can recognize you in public compared to thousands of other real estate agents then you have successfully set yourself apart from your competition. You may be surprised to learn that sometimes when your customer base or clientele doesn't recognize you, or perhaps even sees you as much different in person than what you represent publicly, you could unintentionally create distrust among them. Think of some of your favorite celebrities. Have you ever been super pumped up to meet him or her? Only to find out that celebrity is not as friendly, funny, or humble as you imagined? Were you let down? Did you lose interest? As you build your image, you must be mindful that your audience will expect congruency in representation. They expect to meet the person they see on display in the public arena.

If you are building your image the correct way, your future prospects will view you with "celebrity-like" appeal. For this reason, you will want your pictures, persona, and appearance to be recognizable. That means new business cards and new photos! No more outdated photos or "glamor shot" headshots on your business cards and social media pages. Your image should represent you with 90% or above accuracy. This means you can be recognized at the grocery store, which is a good thing by the way! It may surprise you, but if you are recognizable people may come up to you, spontaneously, and say "Hello!" This is a great thing! Especially if you have a large social media following, your 'social media fans' also known as friends and followers will be excited to meet you in person. Your friends and followers will remember your face and/or name, so make sure your image is aligned with what you represent publicly.

When building your professional image, the goal is to be different than every other agent but also true to yourself. Of course you can add in a little "glamorous flair" if you choose to.

TIPS ON HOW TO BUILD A MEMORABLE PROFESSIONAL IMAGE

1. Build up confidence in your look

Confidence boosters can come in many forms. You may gain confidence by losing weight, may be switching up your wardrobe, or even donning a new hairdo. Feel free to decide whatever you are most comfortable with. For me it was all the above, I lost a few pounds, changed my hairstyle and even bought a new dress! These simple changes boosted my confidence way up and it showed in my pictures and in my energy. I started happily sharing my successes and photos all over Social Media and I was charming to meet in person. Those positive experiences led to even higher levels of gratification. An affirmation I always remember is when you look good you feel good, and when you feel good, you do good.

2. Mind Your Manners

In public, be friendly, be approachable, speak kindly to others, be professional, smile as much as possible, you never know who is watching. Your next client could be standing behind you in line at the grocery store, or she could be lady next to you at the nail salon, or he could be introduced to you at a networking event by a friend. You never know where your next lead is coming from, so always be mindful of your manners. People will remember you and how you treated them when they met you in person. Remember, first impressions can sometimes be lasting impressions.

3. Hire a Professional Photographer

I cannot emphasize this enough, your pictures matter! My pictures have taken me so far. I am forever thankful for the decision to get high quality photos. Get pictures that are high quality can be posted online and in print. Make sure you select a neutral background for your photos. Avoid selecting an object or scene in your backdrop, or an on odd color i.e. purple wall. The only exception would be of course, if the object, scene or odd color background was a part of your brand strategy. Choose photos that can work for any type of marketing. Remember, you can add your picture to postcards, magazines, business cards, Facebook ads, Guest Speaker panels, networking fliers, Chamber of Commerce websites, banners etc. Choose various photos that bring out your personality. Also, make sure your photographer uses good lighting.

4. Be Attractive

People like to work with attractive people, I wish I could I say it in a nicer way, but the truth is the truth. If you can be attractive on your pictures and in person, that's a winning combination!

5. Hire a Professional Makeup Artist

A beauty tip intended for women, but anyone may apply this tip as applicable. First, let me say I am proponent of natural beauty! However, presentation is everything. When having your headshots or photos done, it will be helpful to have a Professional MUA artist at least "beat" your face for your professional photo shoot. After that, choose makeup at your own discretion.

6. Have a Professional Photo Shoot

A professional shoot is essential for marketing yourself! With quality photos you can put your photo on billboards, postcards, fliers, websites, social media and even thumbnails for videos. It's important that you have a transparent background or simple background so that your photograph can be easily applied to various types of marketing deliverables. Don't limit yourself to "headshots" at your professional photo shoot. Choose to bring props. A few suggestions would be a Just Listed sign, Just Sold sign, Open House sign, etc. Pick more than one type of headshot, try a sideways shot, book cover shot, serious look, funny face, smiling face, big smile, small smile, etc. Have fun at the shoot! Take advantage of your camera guy, it's your day to feel like a celebrity!

7. Dress Better

Your clothes should always reflect you. Use your attire to communicate to your clients who you are as a professional real estate agent. If you choose to go super casual, I suggest you be above average with your knowledge and expertise. A casually dressed professional has to be even more convincing with expertise and skill because you will need to convey professionalism in your communication if it's not showing up in your attire. If you choose professional attire or high fashion you will turn many heads and some clients will be drawn to you for your looks. Take this as a compliment and run with the opportunity to impress your audience. Don't disappoint them, make sure you know the real estate basics and a few market trends. If you dress well and know your stuff, you will leave an impression and be memorable! Get ready for referrals and leads to start flowing in by putting your professional foot forward in your appearance. A few more important tips: always be neat and polished, be casual chic if you must. Always look reasonably put together. Remember, people like to do business with attractive people.

8. Make Public Appearances

Now this works well, if applied properly. A "public appearance" is an inside joke, I use to describe going to networking or professional events. It's my own personal view of how I see the art of networking in a broad spectrum. A successful public appearance should be like a mini celebrity event. Meaning if it goes well, people will be happy you attended and happy they had the opportunity to meet you. For this reason, you should always have a good 'showing', consider yourself in character and your appearance is part of the act. Staging is another personal insider that I used to refer to your professional attire or "costume". It's a good idea to look the part of how you want to be viewed as a professional. Your hair should be well-kept, your makeup should be complete, and your wardrobe should be appealing.

For women: If you go out and you get many compliments you have had a successful "Public Appearance". This may sound shallow, but the reality is we live in a shallow world. People pay attention to looks regardless of what they may believe or say they believe in their hearts. I am sure we all would like to believe we are not "those people", but inside each of us there's a "Shallow Hal".

For men: You will know you are working this strategy correctly if people are naturally navigating toward you and begin to start conversations with you. If no one approaches you at your Public Appearance, walk up to a crowd and see how you are received, if you are welcomed in and your time is extended with this unknown group of individuals you have "worked it". If people are politely acknowledging you, but the impact of your presence is minimum, you will likely need to improve your image or be more open in conversation. An easy way to improve your "image" at any point is by updating your wardrobe, cologne/fragrance, hair, conversation or personality.

9. Be Prepared to "Talk Real Estate"

Real estate is a hot topic at almost any event. People love to ask things like "how's the market?". Perhaps, they may even know someone who's just moved or is thinking of moving. Maybe someone has a friend that's just bought a house. No matter the circumstance, everyone loves to be "in the know" regarding real estate. Be prepared with information to share, let your audience lead how you respond if you are at networking event. Allow individuals to ask you questions.

At events, don't push real estate down anyone's throat. Refrain from coming off to salesy with questions like "do you want to buy a house?" Let your audience naturally inquire about you and get to know you, they will usually ask you a few test questions to see how knowledgeable you are, be ready! You want to be able to answer these test questions with high marks, the person asking could be your next lead or a referral of your next lead. Every real estate agent should be prepared for questions like: "how's the market?", "how long have you been in real estate?", "do you work with buyers or sellers?" and "which area do you work?". Make sure you have these answers ready to roll out in a professional and concise manner. Remember, professionals are prepared.

10. Have Professional Business Cards

When attending a networking event, your business card is a selling point. Make sure you have a WOW factor card! Your card should be thick, durable, professional, have a great photo and have a call to action or memorable slogan. Professionally, I think it's a good idea to have a matte finish over a glossy finish. Occasionally, you will meet someone that does not have a card on them and they will want to write their information down on your business card, a matte finish will allow you to do so.

As far as having a professional image is concerned, there are many factors that need to come together for congruency. The consistency in your image will eventually develop into what's called your "brand". Once you have an established brand you will begin to be known for distinguishing characteristics such as being a "well-dressed" agent, a knowledgeable agent, or the agent with the red tie, etc. These characteristics give you an advantage over other agents in your market. It will serve you well to create a memorable professional image. Your image should not be focused on impressing others or keeping up with the Joneses. Having a professional image or memorable representation is simply a way to present your best self to the world and to attract prospects to work with you. People like to do business with people they know, like and trust. I encourage you to package your image in a way that makes you unique. Then go show up and show out at places where your uniqueness be well received by people who will want to know, like and trust you. Earning six-figures will be a result of presenting yourself well.

CHAPTER 5

CHOOSE A NICHE OR SPECIALTY

"If you want to make more money, help more people." — *Zig Ziglar*

When I first got into real estate, a mentor told me to pick a "specialty". I thought, a "specialty"? How will this help me make money? Won't I miss opportunities to work with all buyers and sellers? I want to work with as many people as possible. I want to make money, so I will go wherever the money is and work with whomever I need to, to make money! See my mindset was limited, I heard him saying "specialty", but I was thinking "limitations". Looking back now, I see where I missed the mark by not looking for niches sooner.

A niche is described as cornering a market, while a specialty is likened to having a specific focus. Unfortunately, I learned the value of a specialty/niche, after tons of denied applications from renters and cancelled appointments from unqualified buyers. Not focusing was hard, I felt like I was always all over the place. I couldn't service any client to the best of my ability. Being lost in this industry could be a tough game. In real estate, not knowing your audience or who to talk to each day, kills your drive. You need momentum to push through each day. Today, I would say that a focus is a necessary component of your real estate sales career.

Many real estate agents don't recognize the vast opportunities for us to specialize. Think about it for a second. There are many categories that your next real estate sale could fall into. For example, maybe you have a divorced family in your network that may be thinking of selling? There are opportunities available for real estate agents that specialize in splitting residential assets when families divorce. Perhaps, you have a friend that works in Human Resources, maybe his or her company relocates employees every quarter. As a real estate professional, you could specialize in relocation real estate.

The truth is it's easier to make six-figures once you have identified who you are going to sell your service to. If you specialize and dedicate your business to working with first-time home buyers, this makes your business planning, marketing strategies and research easier. For an agent specializing in first-time home buyers, you should know you need to provide tons of information on the home buying process. It may be best to consider the idea of hosting Home Buying Workshops to aggressively target this core group of buyers. On the flip side, if you are staying away from first-time home buyers and want to work with relocation families then you should know you will need to start going to events and seeking resources where relocation buyers and sellers will need your service.

Some questions you may want to consider as you decide to specialize or identify a niche market are "how can I best serve this group?", "what information or service is the group lacking?", "where can I develop relationships that serve this niche/specialty?"

Focusing on a niche market creates opportunity because you have a specific target to go after instead of serving "everyone". Good example of a niche may be focusing on "foreclosures". Even though, it may seem challenging at first, keep in mind that people buy and sell homes for many reasons. Let's dig a little deeper to fully understand the value of having a specialty or niche. Start with looking at the "buy side" of real estate.

There are all kinds of buyers. There are "investor buyers" who only buy homes for pennies on the dollar. Investor buyers are looking for "deals" so they are usually buying very inexpensive properties sometimes as low as $50,000 depending on your market. Would this be your ideal buyer? Have you run the numbers to see how many commission checks you would need each month at this price point to meet your six-figure income goal? Before targeting a specific type of buyer decide if working with that buyer exclusively as a niche/specialty will yield you the income you desire.

On the flip side, you can work with sellers. Families sell homes for many different reasons. Here are some scenarios of when a homeowner might need to sell: damaged property, financial trouble, moving away, natural disaster, divorce, death in the family etc. As a real estate professional, would you consider selling a home that was damaged by a natural disaster or fire? Would you consider selling an outdated home where the seller did not make any upgrades? Do you want to sell pretty houses only or are you open to houses that need work and repairs? Maybe the seller is upside down on their mortgage and needs to sell their home to escape financial trouble, would this be a listing that you would feel comfortable taking? Targeting specific types of clients makes your work easier and the ability to sell your skills easier as well.

Think of the real estate agents in your area, some of them have dedicated their entire business to handling a specialty market or niche market. Are you in competition with that agent? Perhaps you can enter the market as a newcomer but it would take you some time to gain ground if your competition has built a strong presence and brand in a particular category. I have found that having a focus in your real estate practice decreases the urgency to compete with every agent around you. At the same time, a focus in your real estate practice provides an opportunity to develop your skills. Think of it this way, if you ever did need to go toe-to-toe with another agent for the same customers in the exact same focus area, you would have a fairer chance at winning against one other agent doing the same thing as you, opposed to competing against 1,000 other agents that are the same as you. When all agents are the same, the competition is much stiffer. The odds are in your favor at competing to be 1 out of 2 versus 1 out of 1,000. Dare to be different, find a focus area or specialty.

Chart: Possible Ideas for Niches and Specialty

NICHES FOR BUYERS	SPECIALITIES FOR BUYERS
Newlyweds	New Home Buyers
Credit Repair	Investor Buyers
Renters	First-Time Home buyers
Generational Buyers	Military Buyers (VA Loan)
Relocation	Entrepreneurs
NICHES FOR SELLERS	**SPECIALITIES FOR SELLERS**
Builders	Foreclosures & Short Sales
Generational Sellers	Vacant Home Owners
Relocation	For Sale by Owners
Geographic Farming	Expired Listings
Rehab Investors	Probates

You might consider using your hobbies as a way to identify a niche market. Make your life and real estate business fun! Don't be afraid to have fun while you work; if you go to Yoga every Tuesday night, everyone in your Yoga class needs to know that you sell real estate. If you have 5 a.m. CrossFit, everyone who attends your CrossFit class with you needs to know that you sell real estate. Your hobbies could be your first opening into creating a niche market for yourself. A great perk for adding your hobby as target group is because it's highly unlikely other real estate agents will be participating in the same activities as you, so naturally there is less competition! It's highly unlikely you'll see another real estate agent in your cupcake cooking class with you on Saturday mornings or hiking up mountains or whatever activity you like to do in your spare time. Still not sure where you can focus your real estate practice? Consider taking up a new hobby. You may gain more business to reach your six-figure or more income goals and have fun at the same time. That's an all-around win!

CHAPTER 6
SELF-PROMOTE

"Aim to provide helpful resources, and form honest connections. No sales pitch required!" — Kimberly Haydn

t can't be expressed strong enough how important it is to share with everyone you know that you are in real estate. As a real estate professional, my business has literally come from everywhere. From Instagram Posts, Facebook Messenger communication, my LinkedIn Profile, referrals from members in Professional Associations, Open Houses, For Sale by Owners, and my sphere of influence. You may not realize it but you "touch" people everywhere you go. A wonderful thing about life that we can all benefit from are the "laws of attraction" and "6 degrees of separation". We are all just a connection or two away from someone that can help us change our lives! I know it may sound kind of corny, but I promise you there is someone waiting for you to be successful. Les Brown speaks about having greatness within you, I truly believe this! If you don't know who Les Brown is I certainly suggest you look him up. Overall, he and many other highly successful people believe it's your duty to live up to your full potential because you don't know who you may inspire!

Promoting yourself as a real estate professional should be an honor if you love what you do and you are happy to be doing it. I know we are all concerned that we will be "bugging" people with our constant promotion. However, the truth is all of us come from unique backgrounds and experiences, so someone in your circle may be inspired by your journey. Your ability to effectively express what you do, your motivations, your successes, your failures could be just the inspiration a close friend or family member may need. The way social media is set up these days your story could inspire a total stranger.

The real goal of self-promotion is to get more business! People buy from confident go-getters. When you are actively promoting yourself your prospects will take notice. Of course you'd want to promote yourself in a way that is not overbearing.

I'd like to take share a few ways as to how I promoted myself and what worked to gain more business and more income.

WAYS I SELF-PROMOTED & BUILT A NAME FOR MYSELF

1. **I started a Young Professionals Home Ownership Series—** This was a first-time home buying workshop for professionals 25-40. I had at least 10-20 attendees attend each class.
2. **I talked to people—** I attended as many networking events as possible, I sparked up conversations with strangers, I handed my business cards out and I followed up regularly by sending them an email. I added all the people I met to a free newsletter database offered by my local real estate association.
3. **I openly expressed myself—** Don't be afraid to let your inner personality out. For me, I used my social media profile to speak up regarding controversial issues that affected my hometown. This resonated with several people and helped me to increase my social media presence.
4. **I created attention for myself—** I started being active on Social Media by posting 3-5 times per day, I always shared motivational quotes or pictures of me living my life in a fun positive way. Like-minded individuals were drawn to me and still seek out my advice to this day.
5. **I supported others—** If there is one thing that I can say I do extremely well that is championing greatness. If someone has a great idea, product or service, I will openly support and

promote it with excitement as if it were my own. I get super excited for the success of others! I make sure that I support individuals I am inspired by. Believe it or not, when you support others, you indirectly get support back. It may not be from that same person, but maybe someone that follows you or follows them. Like starts to attract like and soon you will have a new group of friends and potential prospects.

WAYS TO SELF PROMOTE WITHOUT BEING OVERBEARING

1. Host Workshops

This will take some creativity on your part to come up with ideas. The toughest part of this task will be creating a concept that's needed but not saturated by other real estate agents already working the same angle. In my market area, home buying workshops are overdone in my opinion. I think a great opportunity would be to create an online webinar where buyers can simply watch the seminar online without physically going to a location. This allows the buyer to start and stop the webinar at their leisure. Hosting an event or workshop is a great way to get your name out. Hosting gets your name on the flier, maybe your picture as well. If you promote the event, people will see your name on a regular basis and become familiar with you. In real estate, people need to know who you are, so the more exposure you get, the better!

2. Talk to people

I know you may be thinking, duh. But this is not as simple as you may think. I once overheard someone say that real estate is a "talk to people" business. I don't disagree. One thing is certain, you will be given plenty of opportunities to speak as a real estate agent. Take advantage of each opportunity presented. When you attend a networking event, your local chamber meeting, or if you are invited to a career fair, etc. use that as an opportunity to "talk to people" and tell everyone what you know about real estate. I recommend attending free and paid events so that you can meet many different people. Obviously, if you can attend an event specified for your target client, that should be a no-brainer go-to event. Also, consider sponsoring events or signing up to be a vendor such as credit repair workshops, school events, professional or business events, etc. As a sponsor, you often have the opportunity to "talk to people". Usually as a sponsor or vendor, you might have a booth or an opportunity to speak for 5 minutes about yourself or your business. Use that opportunity to sell yourself. Having a booth creates more attention because potential buyers and sellers will walk right up to you, you don't have to go out and find them. It's always a good idea to get in front of your specific clientele if possible. It helps if you have a specialty or niche because then you can decide which sponsorship opportunities will be the most beneficial to you.

3. Teach or Speak about real estate

The easiest way to retain information is to teach it. Ironically, teaching helps you refine your knowledge while at the same time provides an opportunity for you to promote your services as a real estate professional. Have you ever taught a home buying workshop? What about a class on money management or budgeting? Have you ever done a YouTube video on things a seller should know before selling their home? Where can you find opportunities to teach? Perhaps you can volunteer for a local community organization, or a nonprofit. Speaking or teaching an audience complements the real estate profession well. The ability to teach or speak creates many avenues for real estate professionals. Don't shy away from the tougher topics.

Remember, people love to learn about real estate. Find topics that you can teach that interest people. Be a little dramatic if you need to be. Perhaps, you could dispel a common real estate myth, or even tell an industry secret that most agents know, but keep from the consumer. Here's a tip when you share information packaged as 'secret' or for 'insiders' people become suddenly interested. You may use this strategy as a way to self-promote your knowledge and expertise.

4. Have High Energy

Everyone notices the person that walks into the room smiling! Your smile is often your first introduction to everyone you meet, so offer it when you are at networking events, business luncheons, professional conferences, and even the grocery store. With a big smile and enthusiasm, most people will be naturally drawn to you. Even if they are not normally enthusiastic, most people will pretend they are if your smile and excitement is bright enough. Most people will pretend at least temporarily. Don't overwhelm your audience, pay attention to body language to see if they are moving toward you or away from you.

High energy helps with self-promotion because it's an instant differentiator. Most people are not smiling or are not excited about life. I know it may sound weird but think about your typical day, are most of the people you encounter friendly and excited to meet new people? Probably not, so believe it or not just being excited about life can help you stand out in a crowd. Consider events you have attended in the past, usually in a crowded room you see people standing around and making light chatter. The moment someone enters the room with a bright smile or big voice everyone notices. Eyes and heads turn, the attention shifts to that person. Be that person that gets the attention! Careful, I am not saying to go into a room yelling for attention but create the ability to walk into a room confidently and with a presence that gets you noticed. Usually, a smile and eye contact is your best opening for getting attention.

A few good places to show your personality are community functions, in a promotional video, or in a public setting. As a real estate professional, eagerly volunteer so that you have opportunities to meet potential prospects! When volunteering, be energetic and make people feel excited when you show up. Allow your presence to create an energy where people inquire about you and ask "who is this guy/gal?" Your energy should be so high that there is tension build up after you leave. That feeling that everyone was soaked up in your presence and when you left the life also left out the room. That's the type of impact you want to create with high energy! If you can feel your audience hanging on to your every word or a slight linger for more at the end of your conversation then you have very high energy. A good goal to set is to get people talking about you in a positive way when you leave a room. Leave every one you meet with a "warm and fuzzy" feeling about you.

5. Support Others

You can support others by purchasing their products, sharing their work, attending their workshops or classes, signing up for coaching or even just simply congratulating them on their success — this cannot be emphasized enough, because when you support others they will support you. I have connected with phenomenal businessmen and women because I supported them when I saw them doing well. Consequently, the businessmen and women whom I have supported with good intention have also supported me. It becomes a cycle of positive reward. You may be familiar with the Law of Cause and Effect that says what you send out into the universe comes back. This could not be truer in terms of providing support to others. You may be surprised to learn that genuinely supporting others helps with self-promotion. Self-promotion occurs because the individuals you are supporting start to recognize you and your brand. Did you know that highly successful people often know who their supporters are? Highly successful people spend a lot of time ensuring they are contributing to the world and adding value. Oftentimes, they track their audiences for business goals and to see what more can they offer as a benefit to their audiences. Since, they are always focused on adding value to their audiences they often actively watch to see who are their followers and supporters! Think of how often you hear celebrity "clap backs" or fans that are now "on the team" of someone they were following just months before. How do you think these random people are getting selected out of thousands of people? It's because as you are watching and following someone is also watching you. If you engage with highly successful people there is a strong chance they will remember you. So support them and show them that you receive value from what they share, contribute or create. If you engage enough or become a frequent supporter, eventually, a time will come when they will publicly support you as well. Their support could come by way of an invitation to a speaking engaging, a repost on their public social media, a connection to a key resource in your market, or even a referral. So promoting yourself through supporting others could be highly beneficial to you. Another point to consider is that when you support highly successful people you create instant credibility for yourself. Showing support for an extremely successful business woman or man will get others to say "ah, okay I see the type of people you follow". Once your audience makes the connection that you listen to, learn from or follow success they will automatically associate you with high quality, leadership, and success as well. Everyone loves a successful person. When you show the world that you appreciate success, people will start to naturally navigate toward you.

6. Celebrate Work and Success

Don't shy away from celebrating your success and efforts! Show your sphere of influence that you are actively working on your craft. If you are door knocking, shoot a quick video on your phone to show how you are creating business for yourself. If you are hosting an open house, shoot a quick video at the house or post your activity on your social media. If you are going to a real estate conference or taking a class to learn about the real estate market, post this information on your social media. Send an email to your database after you have learned something new. Share with your audience how what you have learned can benefit them. Give your network a sneak peek into your personal life, share your travel stories, birthday parties, happy hours etc. so that your prospects can relate to you outside of business or real estate. Do not be afraid to show your sphere of influence how you spend your free time or how you take time to learn more about your craft. Another good way to celebrate your success without appearing to brag is to post your closings. Post with a conscious. This means post something positive about the client that is closing, take the focus off of "look at me, I am REALTOR® that just sold another house". Instead, focus on your client by saying "We closed! It was great to help Maria and her family buy their first home, now each of the kids will have their own room and plenty of room in the backyard for the kids to play during their annual 4th of the July cookout!" When you share information like this everyone is excited!

Your clients are excited, their network is excited it creates positive energy and everyone learns about you. Ask for your clients buy-in to help celebrate! Remember your success is also their success.

Self-promotion is about getting out there. Make people aware of who you are, get to know people, tell them your story, why you're in real estate, what's driving you, and what you can help them achieve. Don't limit yourself to only sharing what you do with family and friends, make connections all over. You have no idea where your next lead will come from, it may surprise you so always promote yourself.

CHAPTER 7
EDUCATE YOURSELF

"It's what you practice in private
that you will be rewarded for
in public." — Tony Robbins

T rue story, when I first got licensed I was a little hesitant to talk to people about real estate because I didn't feel confident enough with what I knew about real estate. I certainly didn't want to embarrass myself and say something stupid. My insecurity prevented me from having many necessary conversations with possible buyers and sellers. I'd like to remind you that buyers and sellers are everywhere, even places you may not expect. Therefore, you must always be prepared to talk real estate and know your current real estate market. Let's look at a few approaches to help you get educated on what's happening in real estate so that you can be a valuable resource for buyers, sellers and possibly even real estate investors.

Personally, I've studied 400+ hours in real estate education outside of licensing coursework. I currently hold 4 certifications in what I would call "specialty" practices of real estate. Daily, I aim to spend at least an hour a day watching a YouTube video or listening to a real estate podcast. I read every night for 30 minutes on business and real estate. If you were to do the math on that. That's 1 hour a day x 365 days a year equals 365 hours of real estate study plus an extra 30 minutes of reading x 365 days equals 182.5 hours added hours of real estate and business study. In total, I am looking to earn 547.5 hours of education each year this does not include conferences, classes or local continuing education classes offered in my area. I am mentioning these numbers because I believe anyone can apply this study method to their daily routine. I must admit sometimes I do not have time to read or watch a video but I do have time to implement one component of education. Adding a component of real estate study to your regular routine will give you the confidence you need to speak about real estate in a knowledgeable way. After you have read, heard and seen the same topics covered again and again you become familiar and naturally better equip to handle questions and topics that you may have initially shied away from.

HERE ARE SOME WAYS YOU CAN STAY INFORMED

1. Take Classes or Courses

Luckily, in the real estate profession there are many opportunities to learn. One great place to start is with your local real estate association. Oftentimes, they offer classes at a discounted price or for free. Your local association may offer certification classes that are offered on a national level by the National Association of REALTORS®. Taking classes could be beneficial for 2 reasons (1) you become more knowledgeable as an agent (2) you are always up to date on your annual education requirements. Some real estate associations require to have a specific number of continuing education hours each license renewal period. If you take classes regularly, more than likely you have proactively covered your renewal coursework in advance. It's a good idea to check the course schedule with your local real estate association on a monthly basis to find out what classes are being offered. A good association usually offers frequent classes with the class normally being free or charging a small fee. Take as many classes as possible related to your craft. Classes you should not pass up are classes that will help you market yourself as a real estate professional, classes that introduce you to a niche or specialty market, or classes where certification is involved. Obviously, don't skip any free classes unless your schedule is full or you have already attended! Some examples of a specialty class or niche would be New Construction Buyers, Foreclosures/

Short Sales, Veteran Buyers, etc. Only attend classes that you have an interest in you can use the information to gain more business for yourself. A good example of when to take a class and when to skip out on a class would be, if a senior housing class was being offered for free by your local real estate association but you have no interest in working with the senior population. In this example, do not attend a class on senior housing just because it's free. However, do attend that free senior housing class, if you have someone in your sphere of influence that manages a senior facility or you have a high senior population in your real estate market area. It will not matter if you have interest or not if there is high demand for seniors in your market place you need to attend so you can either gain knowledge in that area or find out ways to improve your business for that particular niche market. I would recommend attending any class that services a niche market or specialty market that you are interested in. Don't shy away from online webinars either, if you can take the same level of quality class online or at your convenience do so. Anything that will help you get better at being an agent is an absolutely good thing!

2. Study Top Producing Agents

It's always a good idea to learn from the best. Many of my best practices I have learned with Top Agents in my marketplace. As an inexperienced agent, do not be afraid to connect with the top. You must learn from the very best if you plan to be the very best. Connect with Top Producing agents in your real estate market area. In my experience, I have met top producing agents at Award Ceremonies, industry luncheons, professional conferences, social media, and networking events. Sometimes you may even be lucky enough to work with them on a real estate transaction or you may have a top producing agent or team at your office. Use these opportunities to get to know these agents, build rapport with them and observe what they do. Allow yourself to learn from them. If you don't have any real estate or sales experience prior to getting licensed, I would suggest joining a team or office of a high-producing agent or real estate company in your area. The education you learn from working with people at the top of their game is invaluable.

3. Watch YouTube Videos

Over a 1 billion people use YouTube and YouTube gets 30 million visitors each month. Basically, almost any and everything you want to find out you can probably find video or audio on YouTube regarding it. Real Estate is no different. If you want to learn sales skills, I highly recommend watching a YouTube video from some of the top professionals in real estate. Mike Ferry, Tom Ferry, Kevin Ward, Brian Buffini, Joshua Smith practically anyone you can think of more than likely has a YouTube page. I search YouTube videos daily to get ideas on how to prospect FSBO (for sale by owners) & Expired Listings. There are even videos with agents making live calls. That's right live calls! You can watch another agent that has already mastered the art of cold calling or selling by phone make calls and learn exactly what to say and how to say it. Additionally, there are videos about how to generate leads, host and market open houses, real estate investing, and so much more. YouTube is a great resource for learning how to do the functional aspects of the job for real estate professionals. As I mentioned previously, I would suggest watching at least one hour of impactful video per day on YouTube. I have included a few of my "go-to" channels in the **Resources** section of this book make sure to check them out.

4. Read Books

When I talk to anyone in business, I am always curious to know who they study. I like to ask questions like "who is your favorite author?" or what was the "best business book you read?" In my opinion, this gives insight into a person's business acumen. If they haven't read a book recently, my sensors go up. I wonder how serious they take their business. Luckily for us, our clients don't ask what books we read as a gauge to determine if they will work with us. However, reading is still important. If you are reading this book, I suspect you already know that. Often because we can find so much information from a Google Search or on YouTube we under value reading. Here's what you should know, the best information about real estate are in a few good books, at least that has been my experience. When comparing books to video, books are like a classic experience whereas video is the modern version of real estate. Although, videos are helpful, I must admit they are more of a "how-to" whereas real estate books explain the "why you are doing this or that". Here's an example so you can know the distinction of what you get out of a book versus a video. You would watch a video to learn *how to make calls to Expired Listings*. Ideally, you would read a book to find out *why Expired Listings* are the best prospects to go after to build your real estate business. A book is an invaluable resource when educating yourself on the real estate industry. Many real estate experts have written books to tell you everything you need to know about real estate sales and how to grow a prosperous real estate business. Simply search a title on Amazon, and voilà! The magic is there. I have suggested some key books that you should read if you really want to understand how the industry works.

5. Study Market Statistics

As real estate professionals, it is our responsibility to study the real estate market. Agents that are well versed on real estate within their geographic area, city, or state are by far the most valuable. Real estate is local. Make sure you are knowledgeable of real estate news happening in your area. The fastest way to make money and create value for yourself as an agent is to know your market. Know how many active listings are on the market, know the number of sold listings within the last 6 months for neighborhoods you specialize, know the average days on market for your geographic area etc. It would be wise to know statistics for your area. Do you live in a city highly dominated by renters or homeowners? Do you know if you are in a buyer's market or seller's market? Knowing this information can help you communicate your knowledge to prospects. Imagine how valuable you are to a potential renter when you can thoroughly explain why it's the perfect time to buy a home because there is an increase in the number of single family homes being built due to demand from a 67% renter's market where the renters are tired of paying rent. Picture saying, traditionally our city has a been a renter's market but we have builders, and a local government body committed to increasing home ownership for our local residents. Speaking of real estate in this manner makes you sound like an expert. You can communicate this type of data if you know your market statistics. Beware that the consumer looks to us as the "go-to" experts regarding real estate. Some consumers will expect YOU not economists to make real estate market predictions. You may already have prospects asking you things like "what happens if the values go down in this neighborhood after I buy this house?", "Will home prices be going back down anytime soon?", "Are home prices going to keep going up?", "When is the next real estate bubble?" Wouldn't it be a good idea to have your own opinion regarding this matter that you can share? Sure, we are not economists and we don't make predictions but we can be educated and speak confidently on real estate with our clients to build trust and demonstrate knowledge.

Being educated is about being a better professional. I am sure we recognize that we are in a highly competitive industry, partly because it's an easy industry to enter. However, what distinguishes the competition from the masses is often skill set. Skills in real estate that must be learned are prospecting, sales, business planning, marketing, handling objections, negotiations and so on. The best resource to learn these skills through is education. Get educated if you lack the core skills that give you confidence as an agent.

CHAPTER 8

MAKE A FINANCIAL INVESTMENT IN YOURSELF

"Invest in Yourself, you can afford it. Trust Me." — Rashon Carraway

J ust do it! Make the financial investment in yourself. We all know this at the core of being in business but sometimes we are stubborn about it or on occasion we may not have the financial means to do so. You have to come to terms with the reality that to grow as a real estate agent, you will need to spend money on yourself, your education and your business. In short, you must be willing to invest in you. Investing in you may vary depending on your goals. It's possible that an investment in yourself may mean taking a class for $199 to become more knowledgeable about a specific topic, or it may mean spending $250 on a photoshoot to improve your image. You may need to hire a professional makeup artist for $75 to make sure you look like perfection on your business cards and other photos. You may spend $125 to have business cards designed specifically for you instead of ordering cards for $25 from Vistaprint. Whatever you decide is your choice. Just know that you have to pay the cost to be the boss! Don't skimp on yourself. We learned earlier that your brand matters, your image matters and how you show up matters. When you are establishing yourself in the marketplace as an authority figure, it is usually not the ideal time to be frugal. Don't get me wrong, you must be extremely responsible with your finances and create healthy budgets and spending habits that work for you. No one (not even I) can tell you how much you can afford to spend on marketing, lead generation, business cards, signs, headshots or any other part of your business. The goal here is to simply convey to you that you must spend money on yourself if you are going to be in business for yourself and being "cheap" is not always the best practice. Always spend reasonably according to your budget and the audience you are trying to reach. For example, you wouldn't attempt to sell a million dollar home with a flyer that you made at home and printed on color paper at Office Depot, would you? If you were selling a million dollar listing, I think it would be safe to assume that you would use a high quality photographer to shoot the home, perhaps even have some drone camera shots done to cover the complete landscaping and exterior of the property. You would probably hire a professional Graphics Designer to create a nice brochure to showcase the home. Or even get more creative with other ideas. The tools you would need to effectively market this home would be different than you were selling a $50,000 home that had been abandoned for 6 months. For the abandoned property, you'd probably simply have your professional photos done and items removed from the home. Your marketing budget may be vary for each type of home. You may feel comfortable spending $10,000 to market the million dollar listing while you would only spend $250 on the $50,000 listing. The point here is that your budget will often vary depending on your preferences. Don't be afraid to take the risk of spending money to get a higher quality client. Don't be afraid to take the risk of spending money to get more clients. If you need to purchase a new pair of shoes to compliment your suit for an upscale party- buy them if you can afford them. Need more books on how to be successful? Purchase them if you can afford them. Your education is also a part of investing in yourself. Investing in yourself could include paying for online webinars, attending local professional conferences, national conferences, or even paying a monthly fee for a CRM system. Usually these have costs associated with them if the costs are within your budget or financial means, don't be afraid to take the risk to grow as a professional.

HOW DO YOU KNOW IF YOU ARE MAKING A WISE INVESTMENT?

Before any investment you should assess your financial situation. It goes without saying that you should always invest your money and time wisely. A part of being a business owner is being responsible with money, you need to know if you can afford to make a small purchase or a large purchase. You need to know if you can afford to go to a national conference this year or should you wait until the following year. You should know if you join a Chamber of Commerce how many contacts you need to make in order for the membership to be valuable for you.

As a rule of thumb, before I make a purchase for education for any class I ask myself how will this topic help me make more money in the next 30 days? the next 6 months? and the next year? If the class won't help me grow revenue, I don't take the class. If you're not sure which investments make sense, I would suggest start asking yourself some goal-oriented questions as well.

WHAT IF I DON'T HAVE MUCH MONEY TO FINANCIALLY INVEST?

If you are operating with limited financial resources, you must choose wisely where to invest your dollars. With limited finances you need to make it your number one priority to start investing in opportunities that will immediately start making you more money. Make a small investment that will yield big results. Here are some ideas of ventures that can quickly become an asset (1) better pictures (2) a class under

$50 (3) professional flyers (4) professional looking business cards. A picture is typically a good asset because you can use it for flyers, business cards, social media etc. Have you heard the saying that a picture is worth a 1,000 words? Well it's true with a high quality photo, you can add a quote, add it to flyer, sometimes just even adding an updated photo on social media gets attention. Photos, flyers, and business cards are oftentimes buyers and sellers first look at you as a professional. Use these marketing materials to promote yourself. That makes it a worthwhile investment. Taking a class helps sell your skill and experience. For example, you may attend a $15 luncheon presented by a local homebuilder on what to do when relocating. Take the knowledge you learned in that class for $15 and showcase your knowledge in a blog or a live stream on social media. Now the $15 luncheon you attended becomes an asset and tool in your arsenal to get more business and increase your income. Your marketing material can change the way future buyers and sellers see you. Flyers are going to be the most useful if you have identified a core audience to focus on and you can create a message that addresses a need with them. Use your high quality flyer to distribute door-to-door or on social media

The most important takeaway here from this chapter is "don't be a cheapskate". If you can afford to spend an extra $20-$30 on a book that will help with your business — buy the book, if you can afford to spend a $100-$200 to take a class that will get you in front of an audience that sets you apart from the competition — sign up and pay for the class. Don't wait for free headshots day at the office, hire a professional photographer. Think twice before you let your 16 year old nephew design your business flyer in his high school Graphic Design class — hire a Graphic Designer. Understand that any business will have business expenses, real estate is no different. If you need to make a financial investment in your business to help you make six figures in income. Do it!

CHAPTER 9
SETUP SYSTEMS

"A good system shortens the road to the goal." — Orison Swett Marsden

One thing that you may not have considered before getting licensed as a real estate agent is the day-to-day responsibilities of an agent. It may surprise you to know that as a real estate agent, you have a very 'task-based' role in the real estate process. Meaning agents have many day-to-day duties to manage as a real estate professional. It's a far cry from the glamorous life you see on tv. where agents dress sharp, head to appointments and close deals all in 30 minutes. Of course, to the majority of the world being a real estate agent sounds exciting. Many people imagine agents showing Million Dollar homes and playing hard ball through tough negotiations as seen on tv. But the reality is that real estate is about getting things done. A very long list of "things" to be precise. Before you start making more money and getting to busy, you need to have some systems in place that handles the regular occurring responsibilities of the job of an agent. First let's define what the job of an agent is then we will address systems that can complement each role of the agent's job. In a nutshell, a real estate agent's responsibilities can be summed up into the following (1) generating leads, (2) follow-up & keep in touch, (3) client appointments, (4) pitching/presenting, and (5) filling out paperwork. Not as glamorous as it looks on tv, huh? To make it even more complex, within each of these five elements of responsibility are additional duties that need to be organized and fulfilled on a day-to-day basis. With so many "to-do's" in real estate, you must be highly organized. Setting up systems to automate your tasks keeps you highly organized. The more organized you are, the more money you make. You make more money by being organized because you free up your time. With extra time, you can focus on more meaningful tasks like income producing activities. If you are spending valuable time filling out paperwork you miss out on important conversion activities like a face-to-face appointments. To help you earn six figures right away, I suggest you set up systems from the very beginning. Below is a list of systems that you should have in place along with the specific responsibility it matches.

RESPONSIBILITIES AND SYSTEMS

Responsibility: *Follow-Up and Keep in Touch*
System: *Monthly Newsletter*

As a real estate agent, if you are actively marketing yourself and following the advice in this book you will meet many people. As you meet people, you will want to stay in front of them. The best way to do that is to follow-up by having a routine in place. The simplest routine for any agent is to send out a regular monthly newsletter that goes to your entire database. Sending out a monthly newsletter keeps your name in front of your audience. Where can you get a newsletter from? There are many websites that offer free newsletters to real estate agents. Sign up with a newsletter provider immediately. This will keep you in front of all the potential prospects that you meet. You may even want to include any current and future clients that you may have in the newsletter distribution. You always want to be top of mind as a real estate agent. Another tip is to select a newsletter option that offers professional branding.

What makes a good newsletter?
Some characteristics of a good newsletter you want to dedicate for your clients when you are starting out are:
▸ Make sure the Newsletter has branding capability— meaning you can add your logo, photo and contact info

▸ Have automatic settings — you should be able to set it and go

▸ Quality Content should be provided — the newsletter content should be created by the provider but be relevant to the consumer.

▸ Newsletter should go out frequently — the newsletter frequency should be a minimum of once per month

▸ Upgrade the newsletter — choose a service provider that offers an ability to upgrade or customize the newsletter in the future

You can create your own newsletter or partner with other industry professionals. Home warranty companies, and sometimes lenders, have newsletters that they send out on a monthly or weekly basis. If you deem the content is relevant and valuable to your clientele ask them if you can co-brand with them to send out the information. The newsletter is important because it helps you to stay in front of your clients and your prospects consistently. Personally, I have found the newsletter to be the most valuable tool I could put in place because it changes content every month and keeps my name and valuable information in front of my audience regularly.

Another tool to have in the arsenal is a good CRM, a Customer Relationship Management system. This will allow you to send out monthly newsletters, birthday cards, and mass email messages automatically to your database. You can also promote your Open Houses, Just Sold, and Just Listed real estate deals. A CRM is a requirement if you are serious about making six-figures as a real estate professional. There is no faster way to stay in touch with everyone you meet than by having a CRM in place where you can automatically follow-up each month with your database or sphere of influence.

Responsibility: *Generate Leads*
System: *Public Profiles and Social Media*

To make a six figure income you must work with clients that plan to buy or sell a home. If you do not have active home buyers or sellers ready to buy a home, you must create interest in buying or selling. Creating interest is what we refer to as "generating leads". Generating leads can be challenging for real estate agents because oftentimes REALTORS® are not sure where to start sharing information that potential buyers or sellers may be interested. This is where your public profile can really come in handy to help you get attention from buyers and sellers. Since I have been in real estate, each year I receive at least one lead from my public profiles. There are two great reasons why generating leads through your public profiles are beneficial (1) credibility— if a prospect hires you because they found you in a public search, or they follow you online you will have more credibility with that prospect. Why? In the prospects mind, you have more credibility because they have done the "research" on you, they "looked you up" for goodness sake so they feel more confident in your ability to help them (2) it's free and ongoing— once you set up your public profiles online you don't usually have to go back and reset them unless you choose to. After set up, your profile actually begins to work for you with very little maintenance on your end. It may be hard to believe but setting up a free account with professional headshots and a well-written bio could produce leads that could help you earn six figures. In my experience the worst case scenario has been one lead a year. It doesn't take much evaluating to realize that a free opportunity that produces any dollar amount above zero is a great investment. I liken the free public profiles to free publicity. Think that over, public profiles allow you to publicize your name, photo, contact information and skill to the public for free. You should take full advantage of that opportunity! It's very rare that you will have a chance to get that much exposure at no cost to you.

Below are the top public profiles every real estate professional should have set up so that they may introduce themselves to the world. A fun way to look at your public profile is as an introduction to the world. It's in your best interest to set up this "system" because the world is watching and you never know where your next lead is coming from, a ready, willing and able buyer or seller could be searching online right now for an agent like you!

PUBLIC PROFILES TO SET-UP

Personal Facebook
Facebook Business Page
LinkedIn
Twitter
Google Plus
Instagram
Snapchat
MLS Profile/Real Estate
Association

Realtor Property Resource
(RPR)[2]
Cloud CMA[2]
YouTube
Realtor.com (if you are
a member)
Homes.com
Pinterest
Blogger

Responsibility *Client Appointments*
System: *Automated Calendar*

Another important task to manage as a real estate professional is setting appointments and meeting with clients. It can be quite

2   These are free services in the Houston, TX market, check with your local real estate association to find out if the services are offered in your area at no cost to you.

overwhelming if you are not organized. The easiest way to maintain your appointments is to have an automated calendar system. You can use Outlook, Google Calendar, Calendly, or Google a system that works for you. Bottom line is that you want to make sure you have a tool in place to keep your appointments so that you can spend your time focused on money making activities instead of working as a secretary filling in calendar spots for appointments. Prospects will respect your time if you have a system in place to set and schedule appointments.

Responsibility: *Pitching/Presenting*

Systems: *Centralized Showing Service, Online Webinars, Conference Calls, Skype, Google Chat*

As your business grows, you will need systems in place for many aspects of the business. One area many agents overlook is how they get in front of clients. As a professional salesperson, the more often you are in front of people the more money you make. But who says you have to physically be in front of people? This is where a professional agent can make all the difference! Imagine if as an agent you could use the time in front of your clients to be more convenient for you and them. Even though, the real estate industry is "people-based", a lot of times we are not serving the needs of the people. Our buyers and sellers have varying needs in communication, seeing homes, and meeting with you. Why not create systems that meet the needs of the people we serve? How much more effective would your business be if you could confidently tell your seller's that "I am not going personally drive to show your home to prospective buyers, but I do have a professional showing service in place where a licensed Buyer's Agent can schedule appointments with qualified buyer's at their convenience". Take time to explain to seller's how you are saving them time by using a professional showing service. This creates value for you. On the flip side, seller's will have a better understanding of the showing process. This could possibly prevent some seller's from feeling like you are not doing your job. Your seller could be under the impression that you are going to personally open their house up and show every interested buyer. I have had that happen before, I had to explain the systems we had in place. The seller thanked me for it and felt more secure because now he knew that if I wasn't personally showing his home another licensed professional would. This eliminates the fear sellers may have of complete strangers roaming through their homes. Instead of requesting to meet every buyer at the office consider hosting a live conference with your buyer by phone or video using Skype or Google Chat. Our business is about service right? It's not always opportune for buyers and sellers to come into the office to meet with you. Why not create an environment where you are servicing your customer's needs? With technology we now have more tools to help us do business in a way that is convenient and also effective. If you have buyers or sellers that work crazy hours, arrange a convenient online meeting with them so that there life isn't disrupted for a 30 minute – an hour appointment with you. If you're very organized there isn't much you will say in person that'll be different than what you say on your video call. Besides you will have plenty of time for face-to-face time during your showings, closings, and other follow-up activities etc. Here's another idea, instead of scrambling around town trying to find a place to host a home buying workshops? Consider hosting an online webinar instead. An online webinar will allow buyers to go back and revisit the content at a limited or unlimited time, however you choose to set it up. Pitching and presenting to clients is about building rapport and demonstrating value. Your client's will feel connected to you by the way you handle interactions with them, and your value will be perceived when you put their needs first. With proper systems and management in place you show prospects that you are in business to be effective.

Responsibility: *Paperwork*

Systems: *Zip Logix, Dot Loop, DocuSign, Google Docs, and/or an Assistant*

If you are already a licensed agent, I am sure you have heard of the above mentioned company's before, if you plan to get licensed soon you will become familiar with them. They are electronic signature companies that allow real estate agents to send paperwork such as purchase contacts, lease agreements, listing agreements, real estate disclosures and addendums to clients to be reviewed and signed as needed. Real estate legally transfers ownership through written documentation. Being that our industry is heavily reliant on paperwork and documentation, it's a good idea to have systems in place for electronic signatures to save your clients time. Having an electronic signature company in place also makes your life easier. Would you rather print out ten page contracts and drive the documents to your client for a signature? That's what you would likely do without having the electronic signature company in place. To keep it simple, saving time on paperwork makes you money because it frees up your time to focus on other more important jobs like generating leads. Remember the more people you get in front of the more money you make. Spending time in the office filling out tedious paperwork could cause you to miss out on opportunities to generate more leads. If you find yourself becoming overwhelmed with paperwork, consider hiring a Personal Assistant or Virtual Assistant. Before hiring staff, make sure you have assessed your finances. It may be a good idea early in your career to start tracking, the tedious and time-consuming tasks that you have to do on a day-to-day basis. Even if you set-up a system to handle these chores, think about how would you train someone to do what you do? It may be a good idea to take notes of what you do and how you do it. You can use those notes as a training manual later on.

There are many responsibilities for real estate agents day-to-day, setting up systems handle the workload. Systems in place increases the likelihood of increasing your income. Systems help you move the needle closer to a six-figure income. Primarily because systems allow you to focus on activities that make you money, when you focus on what makes you money you make more money. It's like the circle of life effect. Don't neglect what seems simple and easy to do. Jim Rohn says, "what's easy to do, is easy not to do."

CHAPTER 10
BE TRUE TO YOURSELF

"Look in the mirror, that's your competition".
— Eric Thomas

With about 2 million real estate licensees in practice it may seem like stiff competition among other real estate agents when prospecting for buyers and sellers in your market. You may be wondering how do you set yourself apart from other agents? I can tell you from personal experience, it's easier than you think to be different than other agents. You'd be surprised to learn that by simply being yourself you can make more money than you have ever made, easily exceed six-figures, and stand out from everyone else. I'd have to say this is one of the gems of real estate. You can actually be who you are as a person and still earn a very comfortable lifestyle. Why is that? That's because real estate is a people-based business. You get to work with real people every day. But the secret is you are working with people in their most relaxed environment, their home! Naturally, most people want to be comfortable when at home. So your clients will have a tendency to be a little less pressuring or demanding of you through the working relationship. Quite naturally, your clients will be more drawn to you when they see you are like them or if you are highly relatable. Real estate allows you to build rapport with your clients faster than any other industry because your prospects welcome you into their home life. Think it over for a moment, what are the odds of you inviting your banker over for dinner? What about your Accountant? Sure at some point you deepen relationships with the professionals in your life but usually it's years later down the road. With real estate professionals, most clients are inviting you over to their home or into their personal life on occasion after one phone call or one appointment. As a real estate agent, you have to be prepared to build rapport and build it quickly with your clients. You will notice that if you are likeable, knowledgeable, and can get the results your clients are looking for you will be paid very well.

Unlike other professions, as real estate agents, we don't have strong industry norms that create an expectation in the public's mind about how we should work as professionals. Meaning most of your clients don't typically expect you to wear a suit to appointments, or expect you to have advanced training to sell their home, or expect you to have certifications in addition to your licensing, etc. This creates a tremendous opportunity for you. Since there is not an industry standard shaping how you do business with clients, you have freedom to be true to yourself. Often real estate professionals fail to realize that their true superpower is authenticity and uniqueness. Your personality is just as important to your business as your knowledge and reputation. Why is that? Because our industry is based on people and relationships. You can build stronger more meaningful relationships by being yourself than you can by simply being a "professional". It's proven on a daily basis that the most qualified agent doesn't necessarily get the job to sell a home or work as a Buyer's Agent for a family. I am not championing a right or wrong perspective, I aim to make you aware that being qualified is simply not enough to ensure a six-figure income in real estate. With our industry being largely based on relationships, we must consider how our personal character impacts the relationships we build. I can tell you the best way to demonstrate your personal character is through being genuine. Genuineness is the fastest route to building trust with your clients.

REASONS TO BE TRUE TO YOURSELF

Avoid Monkey See Monkey Do

Following the lead of successful agents is certainly the road less traveled. It makes sense for any agent not getting results to follow the path laid out by other great agents before them. Where the lines become crossed is when you have agents that follow real estate leaders but don't develop into real estate leaders on their own accord. As you follow others, don't forget to develop your own leadership ability. Follow other great agents walk, then develop your own stride. Avoid mimicking too much and not creating your own. When you mimic without creating then you create confusion in the marketplace among customers and indirectly undervalue both agents. The consumer normally doesn't distinguish who was doing what first, agents that lead and agents that copy are one in the same to the consumer, both agents become equal, then uniqueness dissolves. A best case scenario of a copying an agent in your market would be that the consumer sees no distinction in either agent. On the flip side, the consumer could have the reverse action and actually notice that one agent is copying another. Think about what effect that may have on the consumer. A harsher impact could be that the unoriginal agent could be labeled as "corny". If this happens, a real estate agent's business could suffer. Since, your business relationships with clients are strongly built on rapport, your customers are always reading your motives and intentions. If you start running low on ideas or creativity of your own, your customers will start to sense desperation from you. Desperation creates distrust almost immediately. If your clients start to distrust you your business will go into distress. The cure for this is develop your own unique way of doing things so that you don't have to depend on another agent's style. Allowing your originality and creativity to grow will provide opportunities for you.

Get Some Hobbies

Hobbies are true separators, it makes you different from other agents instantly.. Your hobbies are truly unique to your personal preferences and sometimes even skill set. Adding hobbies or refining hobbies gives you an edge among other agents. Use your hobby to attract more clients and build a network.

You Are Your Only Competition

A lot of agents feel the need to go toe-to-toe with other real estate agents for market share, profits and attention. Don't let this happen to you. If you are following anything I am sharing in this chapter you can pick up on the ideology that there is no competition when you consider running your business based off of the right factors. What do I mean by "no competition"? I don't mean that literally as in you will be on the only real estate salesperson still standing while all others have been eliminated. Instead what I mean when I say there is no competition is that there is really no one like you. This is an important factor because in real estate one of the most valuable components of your business is YOU! So if there is no one else on planet Earth like you then ideally there is no competition. However, what most businesses do to make sure there competitors don't affect their profits is they focus on strong differentiation factors. I suggest you do the same. Stop competing with other real estate agents and start dominating with your skill set. Your focus should be on minimizing or eliminating any competition. Whenever you are approached with how are you different? Your answer should be precise. Your buyers and sellers should not even consider another agent competition if you have clearly defined your value. Instead, the consumer should see you as a specialist or an anomaly compared to any other real estate agent. Competition is crushed when you start creating value in the minds of the consumer. For example, when you think of burger joints in the United States I am sure a bunch of restaurants come to mind there's McDonald's, Burger

King, Wendy's, Jack in the Box, In and Out Burger, Whataburger and the list goes on. Sure each establishment sells "burgers", but when you think about it neither compete toe-to-toe for burgers. When given the option consumers choose between charbroiled burgers, old-fashioned burgers, big burgers, juicy burgers, etc. Then there is even further distinction with the toppings for your burger and the type of burger patty you choose or the type of beef. In the end, it's a burger packaged to fit a company brand. That's how your real estate business should be, sure you many have thousands of agents in your market selling "real estate" but what are their specialties? What makes them unique? When you identify what sets you apart from everyone else then you will see that there really is no competition. Your competition is only you. How different can you be? How different are you naturally? What are the things that are unique about you that no one else can duplicate? Do you practice a sport? Do you have a special talent? Are you a natural leader? Do you have a higher level of education than other agents? Do you have more professional contacts? Are you involved in a particular organization? Being yourself allows you to stand out from every other agent. If you stand out, you don't have to focus on competing because your audience already sees you as different. Therefore your differences will be appreciated and not viewed as a tactic to get more sales. Be mindful that the world can be very critical if you come off as unauthentic in anyway, the walls will start to come down. It's better to be an original version of yourself than a carbon copy of someone else. In the real estate industry, real estate agents often lack a competitive advantage and find it hard to compete with other agents in their market thus making it more difficult to stand out among the crowd.

Being yourself is important as a real estate agent be simply because it helps you connect with more people. The more people you connect with personally and professionally the more money you make. To earn a six-figure income or higher you must have a large network of people that you are connected with. People love doing business with "real" people, they want to connect with someone that they can relate to. You can and will build an audience around whoever you are. I strongly advise against sharing derogatory, negative, or offensive political, ethnic, or religious content publicly as a part of who you are.

CHAPTER 11
FIND YOUR TRIBE

"Surround yourself with people who add value to your life".
— Alex Elle

After entering into sales, I learned right away that networking would be a key element to growing my contact list and increasing business opportunities. Being in a new city where I had no history or prior experiences from high school, community, or family I was forced to go out and establish brand new relationships. Initially, like most sales professionals I was taught to "tap into your sphere of influence for warm leads", "keep calling cold leads because it's a numbers game", or don't forget that "your network is your net worth". Well, I was often discouraged by these oversimplified statements because I could not use this as a point of reference to grow my network. Primarily because my sphere was very limited, my network was "co-workers" who were also like me transitioning to a new career and moving to a new city. In order for me to be successful, I had to take a different approach to become credible and stand out among my peers. To build my network, I implemented different strategies that would attract an audience to me. Applying the thinking of motivational speaker, Zig Ziglar, "you can have everything you want, if you will just help other people get what they want" I went out into an unfamiliar city and started developing relationships with people that I did not know.

FINDING YOUR AUDIENCE

To identify my audience, I started identifying unique qualities within myself. I encourage everyone to do this. Take a personal self assessment test to learn about yourself such as the DISC or Strengthsfinder. Understanding your personality and strengths helps you to get along with others better and it helps you understand how to make decisions better. Also, write down your hobbies or interests then strategize a way to start connecting with others like you. When starting my real estate career, I was a young professional so I quickly started joining young professional groups. Soon, I was meeting other people like me and building a network. As a Houston transplant (recently relocated to the city), I forced myself to go out and connect socially. To meet people, I started using websites like "meetup" to find social gatherings. I found events through sites like Eventbrite and I would even go out alone and talk to strangers at "happy hours", "clubs", "business networking events", and "business seminars". All of these forced interactions built self confidence, taught me how to handle rejection, and how to connect with strangers. When connecting socially, I focused on activities that I liked and I even started my own social groups. I made the most contacts when I joined organizations like young professional chapters and social circles. I blended my personal life with business so that I could connect with as many people as possible. A surprising byproduct of joining these organizations was that my natural leadership skills began to show, my authentic attitude emerged, and my spirit of helping and contributing started to get me noticed by people. At this point, I began developing my "tribe" and was able to compile a database of supporters.

YOUR DATABASE IS YOUR TRIBE

As a professional salesperson, you must understand that any person you meet is a potential client. Therefore, when you meet someone being knowledgeable and authentic can generate immediate attention and business. The value of self-awareness is underrated in sales. The reason I say that it is underrated is because there is power in uniqueness and individuality. Instead of competing for clients amongst other agents, your business will be better served working with people where you can establish instant rapport or credibility. For example, as a former school teacher, one major opportunity I capitalized on was ability to connect with schools and teachers. I figured out ways that would be mutually beneficial so that I could add value to teachers (my tribe). I was able to create opportunities to connect with teachers by using my prior understanding of teachers needs. Even though I was not in education anymore, I did not disregard my potential client base. I used my prior experience working as an Educator to brainstorm and create ideas that I would have wanted presented to me if I was still in the classroom. Don't be afraid to extend yourself out to your networks. Those audiences that you may not know personally but you can fundamentally understand their desires and behaviors can bring you long-term business success. Don't overlook the people that you already know. Don't overlook an audience that you can easily access. Don't spend time developing a new audience while disregarding your current audience.

DEVELOPING YOUR TRIBE

Identifying supporters as soon as possible is the key strategy to building a sustainable career as a sales professional. Most professionals identify their sphere of influence as people that "know, like, and trust" them. The best way to connect with your tribe is to be authentic. Authenticity is all the rave especially in today's world where it seems as though everyone is an "influencer".

Everyday people are looking for genuine people that they can learn from and be inspired by. Authenticity has to come from within one's self. This is a skill set that you must develop and master on your own. Unfortunately, it can not be taught it must be practiced and mastered. The best advice available that may guide you in the right direction is to be okay with being "vulnerable" with your audience. Your vulnerabilities show your "humanness" and help complete strangers connect with you simply because you share a similar likeness. For example, get comfortable sharing that you are a new agent, get comfortable sharing your mistakes as a new agent. Don't feel as though you must always be perfect. People love to see and hear about failures and imperfections! Everyday people want to feel like they are not the only ones struggling or making mistakes. Show them that as a professional you are human and are not above making mistakes. Even though I am encouraging you to share your imperfections I would also still encourage you to be modestly imperfect. You want to share imperfections but not total disasters. Avoid sharing mistakes or misfortunes that make you appear incompetent as a professional. It would not be wise to have your credibility judged by others without having complete context of the situation. Some examples of things to share to develop your tribe could be "having a hard time placing a stake and sign in the ground", a "funny typo text or email" to a client such as "meat you at the house at 5 PM". It's human error. We are all imperfect. These are relatable stories that you can share publicly as learning lessons and be able to teach others. Also, stories can give your audience a backstory into the details of your work and let's not forget that stories can also be entertaining. A goal for developing your audience is to get them to like you and always want to hear from you.

MENTORS AND COACHES

Mentors can be a huge value add to your business. I have seen my business grow exponentially with mentors and coaches. Mentors are usually individuals that you admire and are often personal relationships that last a lifetime. Coaches however usually are paid for a service and help you achieve a result. Seek mentors based on your aspirations and desire for knowledge. Select your coach based on results and productivity. Adding these individuals to your tribe gives you a lifelong relationship with individuals that are invested in you and want to see you win.

CONCLUSION

*"You are the only real obstacle
in your path to a fulfilling life."
— Les Brown*

After reading this book, I hope you learned that to make a six-figure income you have to work. Those agents that are knowledge, believable and market themselves are the agents making money. Not surprisingly when you build up your confidence from taking classes and coursework you take your profession more seriously. Consequently others take you more serious as well. Now that you have finished this book, I hope the content in this book and the resources at the end will help you earn six-figures or more as a real estate professional. In an attempt to be as transparent as I can be, I have shared a large number of activities & thoughts that helped me to become a successful agent. When I started I had very few resources. When I look back now, I see many mistakes made. As I shared in the introduction, my intention for this book is to provide ideas and activities for agents that want to work and apply. *How to Make Six-Figures* is intended be a self-starter guide to creating a six-figure income. My goal is to make this content standard enough that it's applicable to all and will fit you no matter where you are in business. In the last few pages, I have included a few of my favorite books, websites, YouTube channels, motivational speakers and a short checklist of all the ideas shared in this book so that you may use them to start making 6 figures!

NEXT STEPS

"Want shows up in conversation,
expectation shows up in behavior."
— Les Brown

The future depends on
what you do today." — Gandhi

1. Schedule an appointment with a Professional Makeup Artist
2. Set Up a Professional Photo Shoot
3. Update/Set Up Your Social Media
   ‣ Facebook
   ‣ Instagram
   ‣ YouTube
   ‣ Twitter
   ‣ LinkedIn
   ‣ Google Plus
4. Update/Set Up Your Professional Online Profiles
   ‣ Get a CRM system
   ‣ Realtor.org
   ‣ Zillow
   ‣ Your local Realtor association
   ‣ Your website
   ‣ Any profile you may have on professional association pages
5. Dress professionally everywhere you go
6. Know the real estate market and be prepared to talk about it
7. Study real estate 1-2 hours per day by watching videos or reading books by highly successful agents

RESOURCES

Book Recommendations

1. *How to List and Sell Real Estate* by Danielle Kennedy
2. *The Millionaire Real Estate Agent* by Gary Keller
3. *The Secrets of the Millionaire Mind* by T. Harv Eker
4. *7 Levels of Communication (Action Guide)* by Michael Maher —
5. *The Book of YES* by Kevin Ward
6. *The Entrepreneur Rollercoaster* by Darren Hardy

My Favorite YouTube Channels

1. Joshua Smith — GSD Mode
2. Kevin Ward — Yes Masters
3. Coach Tom Ferry
4. Mike Ferry

My Favorite Websites

1. Cloud CMA — www.cloudcma.com
2. Housing Trends e-Newsletter — www.hten.com
3. Real Property Resource — www.narrpr.com
4. Ixact Contact — www.ixactcontact.com

My Favorite Motivational Speakers

Tony Robbins   Grant Cardone

Les Brown   Gary Vaynerchuk

Jim Rohn   Jay Morrison

Eric Thomas   Kevin Ward

Darren Hardy

ABOUT THE AUTHOR

Ramonica Caldwell was born and raised in St. Louis, MO. She grew up in Inner City St. Louis city and is a graduate of St. Louis Public Schools. Ramonica obtained her Bachelor of Science in Business Administration along with a Minor in International Business from the University of Missouri— St. Louis. As a young teen, Ramonica became intrigued with real estate because her father worked as a carpenter. She was also motivated to change the "look" of the neighborhoods she lived in and drove by. Ramonica Caldwell moved to Houston in 2007 and worked as an educator for 5 years before getting licensed to sell real estate in 2012. Since then Ms. Caldwell has earned Top Producer for her office, a real estate brokers license, 400+ hours in real estate education training along with 4 certifications in real estate specializations.

www.ingramcontent.com/pod-product-compliance
Lightning Source LLC
Chambersburg PA
CBHW071447200326
41519CB00019B/5652